BECOMINGS

poems

BECOMINGS
poems

AISHWARYA DAS GUPTA

Hawakal
PUBLISHERS

New Delhi | Calcutta

HAWAKAL PUBLISHERS PRIVATE LIMITED
70 B/9 Amritpuri, East of Kailash, New Delhi 65
33/1/2 K B Sarani, Mall Road, Calcutta 80

Email info@hawakal.com
Website www.hawakal.com

First edition (paperback) July 2022

ISBN: 978-93-91431-33-4 (paperback)

Price: INR 300 | USD 13.99

To every *musafir* longing for a home
every heart that refuses to be broke
love and life, and everything in between
coming, going, and becoming

FOREWORD

With growing years, the deadened animosity and the impending doom propelling out of the darkest of times, our very existence feels threatened. We find it hard to breathe. Aishwarya's *Becomings* unleashes a silence; not replete with tragic forebodings but one that makes us feel comfortable. Her verse stands between the opening and shutting of an alleyway; leaving the individuals, the ones glancing through to figure out the thing that remains unseen during the journey. Her untitled pieces do not subscribe to any authoritative mode but are a departure from the same. It isn't random musings but hard-lived experiences that she puts forth with sheer la verve. Das Gupta's profound sense of literature shows if only it were possible for us to see farther than our knowledge reaches and even a little beyond the outworks of our presentiment, perhaps we would bear our sadness with greater trust than we have in our joys. For they are the moments when something new has entered us, something unknown; our feelings grow taciturn in diffident embarrassment; everything in us withdraws, a silence arises, and the new experience, which no one knows, stands in the midst of it all and says nothing. It comforts us. Dealing with the climate crisis, cosmos, anatomy, and queerness, Das Gupta seems to exceptionally weave the love she has longed for. It is not bound by time. Her refugee heart seeks a tune in ruins that have long been abandoned. Timelessness lies there. She translates the time in her own way, to find a destination as Marcel Proust would say— "...is no longer a place, rather a new way of seeing."

Somudranil Sarkar
02 July 2022
Calcutta

A song for the storm which holds the heart sea on
the palm of its being...

❋

The lone November buzz, somehow
hung on the rickety branches of
a marooned December.
January went by in a flurry.
In her mind, it was still December.

Spring crawled like crickets
and departed silently…

The torrential downpour
washed the colours off her graying soul.
September was still far away
like the light at the end of the tunnel.

Steadily, the sunlight whiffed of the ashes of
yestermorning.
Insomniac songs woke her up from
one reality by drowning her in another — starry abyss.

She unfurled her charred wings.
Between a song and a lone buzz — rested October.

❀

I am stuck on a late autumn sunset
when the sky was a riot of colours
my heart rained fire
flowers found flesh
on my parched branches.

I am stuck on a dark October night
joy, like a bubble.
A prick away stood life, while you held my heart
like a glass bead on the precipice of your palm.

I am still stuck on a dizzy October morning
as my favourite song went on loop in my unkempt heart.
And my heartstrings dance their lonely dance
on every lonely evening.

Fragrance of the crescent blossom kept me stuck.
which bloomed in my favourite October.

❀

I shot a word through the loop of light.
It whirred and purred,
somersaulted in my
frozen dreams,
melting away the icy silence.
It darkened,
and danced,
on the precipice
of my shadow.
The ripples of madness
kept me alive
awakening me in
a new dream.

❃

Your fingers
your fiery fingers
freed the flames
freed the frozen flames
fuming on my fleeting body
I became a fugitive wind
following your furtive footsteps
finding a shelter in your fingers
your, fiery fingers.

❀

A gilded lock, worn out.
Its golden key — witheld from sight,
witholds the secret path
to our ancient gold-crusted word
is worth a million untold tales.

❋

Winter leaves her traces
oddly, refugee cases
flaking like dewdrops
dropping across seasons
blooming Spring in blues and purples
its whiteness ripens to the core.
Winter leaves her traces.

✿

What do you do with a heart full of pain?
You dig a canal from your heart to your eyes,
you water the strange withered blossoms
with your tears — the wilting ones
feed on your sad salt
the water floats within their souls
turning into happy clusters.

*

We live in the box of
words. Words. Words.
its corners, sellotaped with blue-grey ticks.
I see you and you see me
through green and white, exchanging slips...
Banned from real existence
exist, still, we in packed boxes...
A virtual haven of safekeeping and dreamy
memorabilia....

❃

The dark loop winds its winnow
arteries, around the solitary seascape.
The dark winds fly away.
Your dark wispy hair
roars like a storm blown
hut in the middle of nowhere.
The crescent stares
from the dark blood night.
A dark howl tears up
the bloodmoonstorm.

❀

The maroon coat hangs on the hook
by the Blue door.
It was our room,
the one, where little raindrops turned to crystal rainbows
where the sound of sunshine echoed in every nook
and cranny.
The maroon gathers dust;
a creeper has curled up its tiny head through
the broken door.
Its tint is just a forgotten memory of blue.
But, the ashes, remain. Reeking of the fire
dancing in overwhelming madness
ravaging through our stories, sharing our scars.
The maroon coat hangs yet
on the hook by
the Blue door.

❃

The scarred stream
stops flowing midway,
stops growing like
an eternal melody.
It plunges into the heart of
earth singing silently.
I remember her Lullabies
in my dreams where the river
resurfaces, rippling like
a newborn wave.

*

Drunk on a stale sadness
evanescent, effervescing
out of the holy trinity.
The ghost of a fallen autumn leaf
the father of a forgotten hymn
the son of every unborn man
bubbling, bursting
crystallizing like a lipstick stain
on our shared glass of life.

❀

Small, numbered leaves
meander into the lost stream
of memory.
Floating in circles
forgetful of the iron fisted branches
that bound them.
Small, numbered leaves
melting like lost snowflakes
goes diffusing,
into the amnesia
of the longest winter night.

❁

Longing for an old melody
echoing through the
crevices of my cracked soul.
A home,
its roof a ruin, the doors and windows
like shadows from a forgotten time.
A name, unreal
rhymes like a love poem
and soothes a cracked-up heart.

❀

The one who sustains us
through churning changes,
sunswept, moonbathed,
dressed in blue and green,
mighty rivers ribboning its tresses
mountains garlanding its dreams.

Your hubris looks at its inertia
basking in the glory of your
successful dams, mines and oil deals.

The Gaia bides its time
patiently until the tipping point will
topple and thwart your arrogance.
Be wary,
you're not saving the Earth,
you're just saving yourselves

❄

The black of your tongue
mingled with the dark sadness of your deep gaze
The black waves lashed and tore away
the last chunk of ground, beneath my feet

My white soul drowned like a rudderless vessel
travels aimlessly on the gypsy quarters
of an unfelt melancholy of the Ganges
drowning in the beautiful blackness of
your raven eyes.

❀

How do you end a flame?
Which attracts the flutter of the coloured wings?
By flinging it across a marble floor
so that it may crash into a million fragments?
By upturning it
so that the oil may trickle down or all at once?
Or like a long stream of a never-ending
hysteric cascade?
By blowing it out or swallowing it whole
or, devouring by chewing its ashen remnants?
Tell me.
Dear reader,
how do you end a flame?
That attracts you to scar and scorch and seethe you.
A torch of torture gloriously heaving its Violet
flames...
How do you end the flame
and not become the same
in undoing it?

✿

A letter encased within third brackets
tucked away in the safest corner
where tainted fingers are devoid of truant time
to toy with, to maul and tear it up
swaying fragments of forgetfulness.

✽

A word within quotes lifted off the language
which is too cryptic to be deciphered.
Sits idle on the stones of a solitary mound
engraved in a loving hand
like the last word in a letter
which hasn't known an address for very long.

✿

A stalemate of sorts
sorted out the distant
echoes of an almost forgotten sunset
witnessed on the precipice of
becoming the forbidden.
A check threatened
to disclose its concealed fangs
heralding the beginning of
my end.

❋

But then she could not fall for you.
All those crimson dusks flew past with measured wingsteps
the wires, gathering time like drops of frosted crystals
tickled, trickled, tiptoed
across the lines on your palm
creating ripples-waves-storms
to be bottled up
in the blue box within the blue chamber of her blue heart
and your Blue being, turning blueblack
With all the words,
and the silences festering within her being
Where would you go?
Where would you hide?
All the Blue walls,
windows, curtains, the blue fingers and the blue lips,
the deep blue ocean of your dreams.
Whitewashed? Erased?
Where will you hide?
All the blue that dripped from your veins,
colouring up
the Blue clouds in the white sky of her nightmares…
All the blue
but she then could not fall for you.

❀

The little one sneaked through
the busy parlor.
Slipping into the high heels
crystalline, crisp, clementine.
The clandestine exchanges raucous laughter
echoed through the airs.
The tick-tocking watches
blended in with the clicking stilletos.
The tiny flip-flops lay in an obscure corner.
Forgotten.
"A trespasser?"
The one in the dark black polished Moccasins, cried out.
"The little one should have known better!"
The crystalline, crisp, clementine heels
weighed a lot more than could be borne by the little one.
The doors closed, screams and silences in voices
The stubborn windows crashed against
The frames screaming out their protest.
The curtains flowed on with all their might.
The women laughed raucously
The clocks ticked on, the stilettos clicked on
The crystalline, crisp, clementine Lost its heels.
The little one never trespassed again.
A black moccasin like all other black Moccasins
always guarded — the little closet.

❀

The dark curtain shrouds time
keeping it from the lumination of eternal delight.
The forests cry out in dried agony
hoping to 'be', one last time—
a predator, a prey, a bystander, a protector,
before the white waves wash the slate clean.

❀

The flight of bats herald
a flurry of gray feathers.
The crooked crescent hangs like
a broken smirk from the rugged twigs.
It quivers. The hazy clouds pass along
floating with the withering dingdong.
The hags stir away while the kittens sing
a long-forgotten ominous song.

❀

To
float up and away
beyond the boundaries of meaning
behind the meadow of Language.

To
bloom like an unheard sound
on the fresh branches of
a newborn tree.

To
fall like dewdrops
on the edges of an ever-forming
being...

❃

The silhouette of
a yestermorn
rustles still
Dune-like
in the heated backdrop
of my desert-heart.
Its shadows char
the edges,
its memory
eats at the mourning
silence.
It rustles still
Dune-like
pouring itself out
into an ever-forming vacuum.

❁

The song of the moon blossom
floated back and forth
hovering over the
cliff of time —

✿

A silence hangs
on that banished territory
yet disobedience
trespasses

❋

And our love remained
like a faint breath of warm air
like the rock within a stormy stream
an island washed over and over
by tireless waves.

Our love remained
like an anchor
even after
the very end.

❈

A poem is a journey,
a tale, a life,
breathing in and out
dancing with sounds
rhyming like a yarn
spooling and unspooling.
A poem is an echoing pain
to whisper in between
the beginning and the end.

❊

A reed beside a river
whispered a song about a whimper and a growl
about grown-ups who are happy
and love to laugh aloud
about dandelions and deliriums
their echoing ecstasy
and the river round the corner
singing endlessly
about songs without words
and ink who don't make stains
a road that winds on
through the same rickety way
about old lovers who sleep together
and wake up next to their dreams
to find the pain has lost itself
in the magic tinted streams.

❁

The sky
the night sky
is a graveyard of stars.
Lighting and alighting
glimmering tirelessly
fading out like the pain of falling leaves
flying past the backyard
floating in a spiral loop
to subside with the dying light
and fly again
into our hearts becoming
a silent light
night sky.

❀

Our fresh breath
mingled
to create the
stale mangled word.
Its ancient texture
rippling with our
shared memory
glimmers
like the Moon set.
I've heard the ancient Bard sing about,
ever eluding my touch...
Its faded slivers
bursting to form the
flaming golden crown of dawn....

❁

The dazed stars
gazed through the gauze clouds.
We lay at arm's length
together and apart
staring back
at the cosmic void
Stone studded
soft velvety
flowing away
with the trickling
sand grains.
Our hazy tête-à-tête ended on a
cloud clustered evening.

❖

My Sadness gazes back
like a glaring stain,
too stubborn to be
washed away.
It whimpers and then growls,
baring its teeth, threatening to
shred the soft flesh into pieces;
but ends up yawning,
and curls up behind
my bedstead....

❀

I let it be —
under the carpet
behind the dusty
bookshelf where my broom
barely catches its breath —
asleep (veiled in sleep).

It stirs occasionally,
like a leaf before its fall.
And then my heartstrings
are pulled to be
played upon.

❀

Falls. Asleep. Behind damp walls.
Resuming. covers up in dust — my heart.

❀

I come back to you
like winter comes back to spring
its last dead leaf crumpled up
tired and forgotten
waiting for the first grass
to soothe its bleak sadness.

I come back to you
to be forgotten. To forget
all that was, is or will be...
to skim through the shallow
of the warm could have beens.

I come back to you like dawn
comes back to sunset
to meet, greet and exist
in our imagined spaces.

❁

What about the unformed,
unnamed, unacknowledged, and therefore
non-existent?
What about all the pain that
you're not allowed to talk about because it was un-real?
It blooms like a flower on the harsh cactii,
flows like a river moving mountains,
burns like a ghost on the swamps,
rains through the parched sandy deserts...
Reminding it of the salty aftertaste of
a stormy ocean that it once was....

✽

Darkness clawed up
the rocky switchback
where the dawn sparkled sea drops.
It's a valley of deadened wishes,
a disgusting frontier
flaking away like the embers of a

forgotten memory

❁

The broken door creaks.
Still. It feels, still
of all the stillness
that refused to melt.
It speaks, still....

❋

Of the diseased shadows
lurking round the corner
hoping to dissolve, to resolve,
to recede into the beginning of the
primal point.

❀

The slippery meadows roll
into the red oceans; the blue moon
blossoms like a crescent scar
across the abyss of the heart-sky.
Myriad waves crash across
the shore of time
receding into
the shadowy depths of eternal
nothingness.

❋

Storm-tossed heart sea
crashes hard
upon the silver strand
of my being.

The crescent scar looks on.
The last raven flies away.
The sea crashes.
Again. And again.

❀

One morning,
I wake up shivering,
shaking the nightmare off my wings,
I look up to the sky. I fly.

One morning,
I wake up as a storm,
dizzy with despair,
in my eyes burns rings of wrath.

On other days,
I'm a wreck,
like the peels of onions, scattered about
lying in an obscure corner of my dark-untidy room.

And then there are days
when I am like a never-ending
melody. A song of bliss. I hope.
I promise. I try.
I'm not afraid to fall.

✿

It just takes a moment, a second, a millisecond, a bump, a jerk, a tone, a turn, a twist, a bend, a fall, a leap, a touch, the feel of a scar, a gaze, a face, a mile, the last mile, the mile, the one which is waiting round the bend, the milestone, with moss covering its detailed scratch marks, engraved upon it by the mighty hand of time, the decisive creeper's delightful embrace, that mystifying mysterious trance, it just takes the moment to trip— to fall— to fall in love.

And then, what happens after that? Do we take a plunge, a dive, a dip, a slide, or is it that we have nowhere else to go. Love then... Is love then like a leash? An ouroboros? A maze which keeps coming back to the same riddle, the one that can't be solved, the insoluble solute, in a solvent of complex factors, the combination of which is nothing short of an abomination, to create a solution out of which is unnatural? Can it never be mixed, mingled, the atoms loosening themselves to hug, cry and crumble, and delve in a deep embrace? It is unnatural then. A paradox of sorts!

XX+XY
XY+XX

And every other variable is doomed to an eternity of being dubbed as no-entities, shunned. But what about the turmoil within the soul, the fire that burns their electrons, and makes the nucleus rupture and pine to reach out?

It's a riddle— a *HEALI** as we Bangalis like to call it.

Let's return to the experimentation, let's rearrange the equation:

XX+XX—heat/electricity—> ?

What happens now? The heat and/electric charge might force the atoms to vibrate faster and loosen their grip on each other and then they'll reach out towards a free space, for a free fall, then they might collide into each other, and what happens then? An identical variable combining and reforming, to become new, or another version of the older self. Perhaps? Can the empirical tools solve the innate complexity of the essentially insoluble?

One may never know the minor mutations, the slight quirks and the mystical mysteries which shroud the functioning of phenomena, how then do we dare dictate, the essential conformity of naturalness— of normality?

Thus, by a corollary XX+XX can produce a "miracle of rare device" for all that we know, because each X has in it a history of rare ancient alchemy, the constitution of which is unfathomable.

By that argument, one may derive,

XX+XX=X/Y/Z/XX/XY/XZ/….

And thus, under certain circumstances X can trip and fall and touch and scratch beyond the surface of the legitimate to embrace and become the inconceivable, the unutterable, the silenced. And rise in all her corporeal glory to become what she was always destined to be. A part of the whole or a recurring error— hanging in time and space— in a limbo of nothingness— a void of sorts weaving with her fragile fingers, the tulle of silence, the yarns of fractured hope, like Arachne, shunned, cornered, abhorred, yet, existing, nonetheless, creeping round corners, weakening the stronghold of the wholesome normality, existing, creating, falling, rising, weaving, dreaming, daring, dreaming, daring, dreaming….

**heali: riddle or conundrum.*

❋

The ground beneath my feet
trembles
revealing
tufts of drudgery,
sparse vegetation of human sin.

The fistful forests slumbering in fitful sadness,
the tied-up rivers, choked in their dammed distress,
rainbow feathers of oily patches
trickling through the glass box
of my dream, every night.

The one star
on the precipice of our shared horizon
precipitates time honoured anxieties.

The one who has always guided us
home
(home?)
has become an echo of the
lost soul.

I stare at the last star standing.
The rest are buried under
thirty meters of charred
smog
spewing
solid
silences.

❋

A ray of sacred sanctity
woven of moonlight
falls on your shoulder
upon my eyelids
falls and falls. And
falls again.

❀

Fugitive tears tear up
my fragile heart, rise
like a breath of vocal silence
heralding the storm
that had once lost her way.

❉

High heels click through
the cracks of my destiny
flitting past the racing sedans,
the empty alleyways, sleeping strays,
the garbage dumps, overflow amidst
the neon-inked poetry etched across
the heart of the metropolis.

Dazzling-uncalled-silent
fairy lights sit in chaos glimmering
in the distant shadow of an
almost forgotten eatery.

The blind fiddler struggles
with his Violin. Notes, opaque
drowning the dead-end of the
deadened alley.

The music freezes,
so does the lights, high heels and sedans.

❀

The storm trails
off the tail ends
of your *kajol* smeared eyes.
I stand
upon the strand, forsaken
by the waves.
Becoming
the storm lashing out
at the heart of the sea.

www.ingramcontent.com/pod-product-compliance
Lightning Source LLC
Chambersburg PA
CBHW020934160726
47993CB00007B/2781